Gemspirations

Praise Poems

Rowena Stenis

WESTBOW®
PRESS
A DIVISION OF THOMAS NELSON
& ZONDERVAN

WestBow Press books may be ordered through booksellers or by contacting:

WestBow Press
A Division of Thomas Nelson & Zondervan
1663 Liberty Drive
Bloomington, IN 47403
www.westbowpress.com
1 (866) 928-1240

Because of the dynamic nature of the Internet, any web addresses or links contained in this book may have changed since publication and may no longer be valid. The views expressed in this work are solely those of the author and do not necessarily reflect the views of the publisher, and the publisher hereby disclaims any responsibility for them.

Any people depicted in stock imagery provided by Thinkstock are models, and such images are being used for illustrative purposes only. Certain stock imagery © Thinkstock.

ISBN: 978-1-4908-2616-5 (sc)
ISBN: 978-1-4908-2618-9 (hc)
ISBN: 978-1-4908-2617-2 (e)

Library of Congress Control Number: 2014902568

Printed in the United States of America.

WestBow Press rev. date: 3/25/2014

Contents

Acknowledgements
Poetry is the Music of Words

I would like to acknowledge my dear husband Tom B. Stenis and my brother Llewellyn Smith for their honest criticisms of my poetry, and their unwavering support as I search for inspiration in everyday life.

I would like to acknowledge my children and their constant reminders of my life's mission: to help spread the love of Jesus throughout my life's work.

I would also like to acknowledge my many grandchildren and great grandchildren, for showing me that love and an endless supply of fun can always bring a smile to a face and a "hug" to our hearts.

A special thanks to my grandsons, Paul and Luke Stenis, for their touching presentation in the Foreword and for helping gather the finishing touches to this book.

And last but not least, I would like to extend a special "thank you" to Gavin and Lauren Goodrich for their endless support and help in creating this book of inspirational and encouraging poetry with their computer and typing skills.

I would also like to give one last "Thank You" to all of God's children and creatures for helping inspire the poet inside me along my journey through life.

May the Lord be with you,
Rowena Stenis

Foreword
by Paul and Luke Stenis

Rowena Stenis, or as her grandchildren fondly know her as Mom-R (pronounced "mom-mer"), has been a powerful influence on her entire family. She dedicated her life to Christ and taught the Christian message with passion and skill to everyone she met, whether family, friend, or stranger.

Some of our fondest memories come from spending one week each summer of childhood at "Camp Gramps," but one incident in particular will always stand out in our minds, because it captured so well the passion, humor and excitement of those times.

It happened on a crisp summer morning in Austin as all the grandkids and kids and aunts and uncles piled into cars to head south to Schlitterbahn, a water park an hour south of Camp Gramps. We kids wore our bathing suits, flip-flops, and T-shirts. In the bright light of morning, we whipped our towels and chased one another across the dewy grass. But we fooled around only briefly before piling into cars. The oldest of us muffled smiles, too cool to show our excitement. Even our parents had extra springs in their steps as they loaded the trunks of cars with sunscreen, insect repellent, sack lunches, and lawn chairs. No one had to tell us to straighten up. We were ready. Rear ends were planted in seats. Seat belts were fastened. Our towels sat bunched up in our laps. Granddad, ever the mild-mannered and patient sage of our visits, started the Subaru wagon where me and a pair of my cousins waited. Motors idled in front of Mom-R and Granddad's house. But there was something missing. We were short one person.

Where was Mom-R?

Mom-R appeared at last, glanced down into her purse as she pushed through the door and locked it behind her. She wore her bathing suit and sunglasses. She checked her bag again, then looked toward the armada of Stenis vehicles idling before her and brimming with family. Suddenly panic filled her face, and she frowned before she looked down at her water moccasins. "There's no place to sit," she said. "I guess I won't go." This declaration rang out for all to hear.

Immediately following and just as loud, our mild-mannered grandfather opened a car door: "Don't be a martyr, Rowena. Get in the car." There was, in fact, plenty of room. Mom-R was beckoned inside.

We may have gotten a little chuckle at Mom-R's expense, but it revealed a quality of Mom-R's that we loved and admired very much: her sense of self-sacrifice. And though some might argue she practiced it to a fault this was another reminder that she did indeed put the needs of each and every one of us before her own. And she expected (and continues to expect) the same of us. The Stenis grandchildren will always hold dear Mom-R's legacy of self-sacrifice.

This body of work captures that legacy, and in every case exemplifies her relationship with God and Jesus Christ. Her goal of spreading the love of the Lord is accomplished here. Enjoy.

Preface

Many people influenced my desire to write poetry. My mother wrote poetry and set a good example. My father was a university Language professor, and the major discussions during our meals concerned words.

My musical training made it natural to think of poetry as the music of words, and see the rhythm and rhyme in the use of words. Several poems were written while I was growing up, but serious writing came later.

Years later, while on an automobile trip with my husband and children in the western U.S., we visited with many of our friends and relatives, so I wrote thank-you notes to them in poetry. Other inspiration came from life's experiences, such as watching wildlife, meeting other people, family, and the effects of aging.

One poem was inspired by talking to a Japanese lady about forgiveness, love, and acceptance. After 50 years of marriage, many people asked for marriage advice, which I explained in a poem called

"Marriage Advice."

My poems have appeared in the yearly publications of "International Library of Poetry" and the "World of Poetry" anthology. A music publisher in Nashville, Tennessee saw some of my poems, and has set some to music and put them on CD's. One of the latest is "Marriage Advice," which says to put Jesus in the center of your life, and pray.

My first book of poetry, entitled "Reflections," was published in 1994 by Carlton Press. Some comments about that book are as follows:

"The desire to write poetry is almost universal. Few, however, capture the art as well as Rowena Stenis…The poems deserve wide readership."

Dr. Harold E. O'Chester, Pastor

"Of all literature, poetry is the most personal and beautiful to read, and Rowena Stenis is a very personal and gifted poet. Her poems tell us her philosophy, her faith in God, her many adventures, and her love for friends. It is a joy to have reviewed her poems for persons of all ages and creeds."

-- Christopher G. Janus, author of "Angel On My Shoulder",
"Goodbye, Miss 4th of July" and "The Search for Peking Man"

Adventures

A Wish For You

Ever onward, ever upward,
Ever seeking our Lord's will,
May you find His loving guidance
For your life with service filled.

Alaska Trip

Snow-capped mountains, forest, friends--
These two weeks, too soon they end.
Northern Lights, worth losing sleep--
Memories we'll always keep.

Learning native stories, lore;
Weather, history, and more:
Creatures, man, how all survive,
Totem poles and art alive.

Nature's beauty all around
As we travel through the Sound;
Hikes we took around the towns,
Through the woods, walked UP and DOWN.

Toured the gold mine; tunnel cold
Yielding bones and ice so old.
Other mem'ries we hold dear
Even though asleep were bears.

How explorers took their chance;
Celebrations: potlatch, dance,
Music, song the native sing;
We too even had our fling!

April 13-25, 1997

Celebrating

Oh there are so many reasons people like to celebrate;
And now I'll name a few of them, and how we operate.
We've birthdays, anniversaries and changes in a life;
And Christmas, Easter, New Year, July Fourth, and gaining wife.

We celebrate a newborn babe, decision, honor, move,
Achieving goals, advancement or blessing from above;
Perhaps a favorite team achieved a very important win,
Someone came home, a business opened, people moving in.

Whatever is the reason that we choose to celebrate,
The way in which we choose to mark each very special date
Does vary greatly with the moods of people and events.
We have a party, shoot fireworks, go on a trip or dance;

Attend a movie, game or concert, hug someone or yell;
Or blow a whistle, play a game, or give a gift, do well,
Congratulation cards, eat out together, have a parade,
Have cake and ice cream, punch and cookies, tea or lemonade;

Drink milk or coffee, milk shake, soft drink (any flavored kind),
Have fruit punch, veggie juice or water, wholesome drinks you find;
But PLEASE don't "celebrate" by putting poison in your bod,
For drugs and alcohol will surely hasten you to sod.

January 30, 2000

Fantasy Airplane

My cousin Joe and I were four.
While sitting 'round with friends and more,
One quest told us a big tall tale
About a plane across the vale.

'twas "in the mountains, in the wild."
So Joe and I, with minds of child,
Decided then to find that plane:
Fantastic, magic--'twas so plain!

We two believed whate'er was told
Because we were just four years old.
Together, out the door we went,
To seek that magic plane were bent.

So, over hill and dale we walked;
While planning what to eat we talked:
Wild berries, grass and rabbits mild
Would be our food out in the wild.

We saw a disappointing sight:
Our big adventure stopped in flight!
Joe's Dad, my Uncle Earl, appeared,
Put us upon his horse, as feared.

He carefully explained to us
The story of the plane was false,
How we must come back home and stay
For safety, love and happy play.

January 5, 2000

Fourth Of July Parade

All the people of our land
Rest from work: strike up the band!
Step right out and march along;
Wave "Old Glory," sing a song!

Homemade ice cream, uncles, aunts,
Cousins, grandmas, grandpas, tents,
Picnics, fishing, boating, trips,
Neighborhood parades and dips.

Lumps in throats from country's pride,
Tingling head to toe inside:
We are proud to celebrate
U.S.A.'s big freedom date.

July fourth we find it's wise
Remembering freedom's sacrifice;
Families gathered, unified:
Freedom's why men fought and died.

July 8, 1994

God Guards

Eight people at home and six shots did ring out;
But God did protect every one--there's no doubt.
Though some shots came close to some ones who are dear,
The shooters of bullets were foiled, it is clear.

Those men who were caught did confess very soon;
Imprisoned and punished by the law it was done.
God proved His great love, and that He's everywhere.
His children He guards and for them He does care.

Events of May 17, 1998

Hold On!

Rain poured in sheets--it rained a lot.
Just two he was, a little tot.
A frantic search as for no other:
We could not find my baby brother!

We knew it as a dry creek bed,
But there we saw his bobbing head.
He'd hold his breath when going down,
Breathing in when up and did not drown.

Beyond his years, was very wise
And saved his life, breathed on the rise!
Our mother found him just in time:
He clutched TWO BLADES of GRASS so fine.

The raging current swift and strong
Well could have carried him along
Beyond where we could rescue him
From being drowned in water dim.

But God was with us in our need,
And cared for baby, prayers did heed.
So thankful we, e'en to this day,
And know God hears us when we pray!

April 24, 2000

Not A Scratch

He enjoyed riding 'round in the country that day
On his motorbike, following winding roadways.
Then the sun disappeared and his lights did not work,
So he hit two guideposts when he missed that big curve.

While he flew through the air, he expected to die,
Falling through that big stickery tree from up high.
For he landed face first on a big pile of rocks
And he could e'en have broken his neck or his back--

Or his head or an arm or leg or his nose;
But a miracle happened, for when he arose
There was not even one little bruise or scratch:
For his dear guardian angel was there, him to catch!

December 22, 1999
Brother Llewellyn's motor scooter accident on
Highway 2222 in Austin, Texas in 1954.

Ribbons And Patches
And Ants

Oh look way down there from so high in the sky:
Now what do you see from far up, very high?
It looks just like ribbons and patches and ants;
When we're up so high there seems even no fence.

Some ribbons are rivers and some are the roads
Following valleys to carry their loads;
And on the road-ribbons we see some small "ants"--
Which turn into trucks when our vision's enhanced.

Upon river-ribbons some rafts can be seen,
And boats of all kinds on the lake, blue and green.
Then what are those patches, some green and some brown,
We see from up high looking down on the ground?

They're shaped in such varied and interesting ways--
The ground shows the shapes as the farmers' farms lay.
So, ribbons and patches and "ants" we can see:
They're rivers and roads, trucks and farms and the trees.

And some of the tall peaks are covered with snow.
We look out the window and see those below.
Now truly, Grand Canyons a marvelous sight;
Behold it down there as you look to the right.

The plane touches land as it smoothly comes down.
We're glad to be back upon God's solid ground.
The ribbons and patches and "ants" become real,
And not little toys, but are big things to feel.

June 18, 1997

Rough Water

We were rockin' and a-rollin' as we cruised there on the boat;
Now that's the really-truly rock-'n'-rolling, please take note.
The dishes were a-slidin' and we couln't walk upright,
But staggered down the hall, and had to hold on very tight.

May 5, 1997
On the ferry in open waters, Alaska tour.

Where Am I

Sturdy granite hills:
Gray and yellow, orange too.
Arbuckle Mountains, Turner Falls,
"Necks" exit to the zoo.
Camping, fishing, hiking,
All are there for you.
What's the state with this to do?

May 22, 1996

Answer: Oklahoma

World Microcosm

Aboard our cruise ship when we visited Greece
Were people who spoke many tongues there in peace.
Together at mealtime all tongues could be heard--
Examples of language mixed and all stirred:

Greek, Persian, and English and German, Chinese,
French, Arabic, Korean, and Spanish, Japanese;
Swahili, American, Australian, and Swedish--
We had our own Tower-of-Bable-like gibberish!

Yet all of the people from those many lands
Had one common goal: to explore early man.
In peace we all came, and congenial we were;
The fun, exploration and learning we shared.

July 22, 2000

Wren Inside

A little bird was in the house;
It flew up high and all about.
We wondered how that it came in,
Discovered that it was a wren.

The time was spring, and wrens build nests,
But inside the house is not the best.
We tried to help it fly outside,
So closed the door to room inside.

We then removed a window screen
In room where it could then be seen.
And next did open window top,
Let wren fly around without a stop.
It flew to curtains and book shelf,
And out of window by itself!

If I had been that little wren,
For freedom, thankful I'd have been!

Amusing

Absent-Minded

Oh, when you look inside the fridge
while hunting for your socks,
Or open up the dresser drawer
when searching for a box,
Or go into the bedroom when
you're going to the car,
You know for sure how absent-minded
that you really are.

Or when you went to find a thing
and then you plain forgot
Just what it was you wanted so,
whether cold or hot?--
Just ask yourself if it's important
that you have it now.
"Oh, well," you say, "I needed it,
but now I don't see how!"

Just take a breath and laugh aloud,
and say unto yourself
That really, truly all you need
is concentration help.
For you're not getting older now,
or "losing marbles" here,
But getting smarter all the time
with fuller mind, don't fear!

What I began to say was, "what…"
Oh, now I plumb forgot!!

Bells

Now bells are used for many things:
To gain attention; joyful rings;
Some serve to help the lost to find,
And others tell the time, remind.

We put a bell on dog or cat,
Or cow, to know just "where they're 'at.'"
The phone that's in the hall
And bell that's at the door do call.
From sick bed, bell can call the nurse
To help the patient not get worse

At Christmas joyful bells do ring
As people happy carols sing.
And bells adorn old "Dobbin's" sleigh
As he pulls us on snowy way.

The bells on clocks, at church, and schools
Keep time, are used by us as tools
To give our lives some special order
As bells outlining time, for borders.

The bells sound very loud alarms,
Alert us to prevent much harm.
Some bells in music makes it pretty,
Give special sparkle to the ditties.

In trolleys bells say, "Please do stop."
In autos, bells say, "Buckle up;:
Or, "Think now, friend, release the brake."
The kitchen timer ends the bake.

But there are "bells" we do not ring:
Bell peppers are some bells, can't sing"
Green Bells of Ireland just look pretty
And so bluebells in the city.

And then there's Blue Bell rich ice cream
Which tastes so good, but doesn't ring.
The Belle of the ball is very pretty,
But she does not make sounds so tinkley.

At Beall's Department Store so big
We find good clothing, e'en a wig.
A bellhop comes when sounds a bell--
To serve when needed, very well.

So some bells make a ringing sound,
But many other "bells" abound.

Mays 30, 2003
Thanks to Llewellyn Smith and Mary Hettler
for some ideas; also Tom B. Stenis

How To Vacation
When Retired

So how to vacation when one is retired?
It could be so boring when one is not hired!
When working so many long years day by day,
We thought 'twould be heavenly to do naught but play.

But some of us fill up our lives with much fun,
And not only that, but for others we run.
For those of us always so much on the go,
Vacation might be just to learn to say "no."

Well, yes, a vacation would be really great--
To travel and have a good change-of-pace date,
Expect that the traveling takes lots of money!
Retirement soon bores some, and isn't so funny.

Or maybe vacation from retirement might be
To go back to work, not be bored and so free.
Vacation from retirement might be anything
That changes the pace for you, pleasure does bring.

December 16, 1994

Hugs

Now hugs are "things" we cannot give
Unless we also them receive.
They make us feel so warm and snug—
Just like a bug in a rug.

I fold my arms around my friends
To tell them that my love I send,
Because they're very special, see?
It's just like loving family.

Of course we hug our moms and dads,
For they are full of love so glad.
We hug our spouses, sisters, brothers;
And also friends so dear, are others.

For friend are chosen family;
And that is true, I say to thee.
We know that all need hugs each day;
So now I send a hug your way!

Hurry! The Maid's Coming!

I'd better clean this house, oh yes,
Before the maid sees such a mess!
I surely don't want anyone
To know how dirty is my home!

If news of this should reach my friends
Down gossip lanes through which she sends
All talk of what a dirty house
I have, I'd be much talked about!

And so, I need to hurry up
To clean the house and fix it up,
To keep my reputation clean
Along with house as it is seen!

August 1, 1992

Mechanics And Dentists: A Riddle

How are mechanics and dentist alike?

Ponder this question to find what they're like.

Both are repairing some thing we use daily--
Our teeth or our autos that must not be failing.
Both do the work with their own special skills,
With specialized tools, jobs they only can fill.
Both must have plenty of bright shining light,
To see what they're doing, to do their jobs right.

Both use their tools while "mouths" open wide;
Both would cause havoc if tools dropped inside!

Idea from Donna Williams

Pet Names

We heard of cat that's named "Chester."
Does that mean he sleeps on one chest, or...
What else could its name mean now--hmmm?
From whence could its name ever come?
Perhaps we should call my dog "Lapster"
Because she stays here in my lap, Sir.

June 10, 2004

Predicament

The ring bearer stood very still at the wedding,
So good and so handsome, though restless was getting.
I noticed he tugged at the best man in front
And whispered a word so intense of some want.

The best man consulted with one right behind;
The word was passed on to the end of the line.
The last man in line shook his head to say "no."
The minister grinned as to say, "Yes, I know."

The minister soon brought the wedding to close
In merciful speed for the child who then chose
To leave as the music allowed him to go---
As gracefully fast as he dashed out the door.

May 18, 1996

Retirement

When we were young we earned our way,
Were always working every day.
While we were raising children four,
We did our part and then some more.

Yes, we were busy, yes indeed--
With home and work and church and deed,
With music, clubs, and school and Scouts,
As we were dashing all about.

But now that we're "retired," you know,
All think we've extra hours and "dough."
Our services, they surely think,
Are free to all, just for a blink!

No matter if we're slower now,
Or if we've plans and dreams for now—
Our time is taken everyday,
Because we give it all away.

However, thankful we can be,
For health and minds and energy,
That we can help someone today,
To lighten burdens on the way.

Retirement time arrived too soon;
But what's "Retirement"-- sleep till noon?
"Oh no," we laugh, "there is no rest--
We're busier now; I think you jest!"

March 5, 1993

The Face In My Mirror

I look in the mirror; and who do I see?
It seems that my grandma is peering at me!
For many long years, it looked just like young me,
But suddenly lately, more wrinkles I see.

The hair of this image is totally white;
She's shaky; and cannot hold still e'en to write.
Her youth, it has vanished and now she is old;
She's thankful to God for past youth; 'twas worth gold.

And now, looking forward to eternity with Him,
A perfect new body with vigor and vim!

The Siren

The siren was squealing and couldn't be stopped.
It started when out of the car we had hopped.
'Twas inside our car and was driving us mad.
We searched for the source of the noise that we had.

We tried all the buttons and things we could push,
But nothing would turn off that noise, make it hush.
We drove to the place where our car had been bought
To seek for relief, but saw that was for naught.

We called the car dealership selling that make,
They said we should disconnect battery, wait.
But that didn't have an effect, not at all!
To another car dealer we went to squall.

Upon the man's face was amusement--a smile:
He made the discovery 'twas NOT a car dial,
But portable radio/siren/flashlight,
Accidentally turned on that made our sad plight!

Embarrassed and happy, amused and relieved,
We were to have finally, silence achieved.
We laughed at ourselves as we headed toward home:
How simple the cure--if we had only known!

April 30, 1998

Too Sick

You see, I'm really very sick:
I need too see the doctor quick;
But then again, I cannot go
Because I'm very sick, you know.

To go receive the doctor's care
I have to FEEL like going there;
So now because I feel so bad
His care today just can't be had.

Therefore, I'll languish here in bed
Until I'm well or maybe dead;
And then I'll either pick me up
Or someone else will fix me up.

July 27, 1992

Wash Day

My Grandma did wash in a different way
When she was a mom in a different day.
At five of the clock every Monday morn bright
She rose up to build the wood fire and it light.

She gathered the clothes and then sorted them out,
Did boil all the whites, punched them down and about;
Then did the pastels in the same kind of way,
And then boiled the dark ones, worked at it all day.

In Grandma's day time, people made their own soap
From animal fat and some lye--and we hope
That never it damaged their skin or eye.
Detergent's a recent discovery we buy.

Before Grandma's day others washed in a stream,
And in my mom's day came the wringer machine
But she hung the clothes on the line out to dry,
And they smelled like sunshine out under the sky.

But now it's much easier doing our wash:
Just sort, put them in the machine and then dash
To do something else while that marvelous machine
Does all of the work for us, gets the clothes clean.

No matter the weather, clothes dry in dryer;
We don't iron the ones that we usually acquire.
Machines do so many more drudgery things
That surely we all seem to live like kings!

December 14, 1992

What to Eat

A necessary habit, eating;
But much we eat is so defeating!
We find that if it's good to taste,
It must contribute to our waist.

Or if not that then what to trust
To be for health, and good for us?
The cabbage types are very good,
But tasty sweets are bad as food.

Some people can't have any salt,
Or spices, wheat (it's not our fault!)
So just remember one thing sad:
Things good for us just must taste bad!

It's hard to find a diet wise
That taste as good as cakes and pies;
But somehow, though, it should be done
So "battle of the bulge" be won.

November 1, 1992

What We Say

What do we say just after a sneeze?
"Gesundheit!" "God bless you!" or "Excuse me, please."

After an accident, belch, or bump:
"Excuse me," "Forgive me," "So sorry for the lump."

If a request you'd politely ask,
Then "Please" is the word, for it's surely no task.

After a favor or compliment given,
Say "Thank you" sincerely; it's rightly proven.

"Howdy," "Hello," "Aloha," and "Hi"
"So long," "I'll see you," "Just fine," and "goodbye—"

These are some phrases to polish talk up,
But what do we say when someone hiccups?

March 28, 1994

Wrestling Match

Who will win?--the man or the map?
This crisp new map gives quite a slap.
It seems to have quite a mind of it own,
Refuses to fold any way it is told.

Instead, it protects with a "crinkle" and "pop,"
Insists on its way of the fold from the top.
The man gives the map a sock and a whack,
And finally wins that fierce wrestling match.

June 24, 2000
Re: Llewellyn and map, while traveling.

Faith

Bouquet Of Eden

They're many bright colors—
Pastels are there too:
Some light and some dark,
And of every fine hue.
They're beautiful "flowers"
On this spaceship of worth,
The jewel that God made,
This garden called "earth,"

The "flowers" are people,
So wondrously made,
Created by Him;
"Live in peace," we are bade.
So this is our prayer:
"may we learn to obey,
And beautiful Eden,
Be God's sweet bouquet."

Inspired by Yong Ae Lee, as we discussed World War II.

Cracked Pots

Like the vessels in the potter's hands, mankind is surely made;
But we are cracked by sins; and so, imperfect we are laid.
Since Adam's fall, through history, imperfect sinful men
Are what God had to do His work on earth, to work His plan.

Now Abraham, whose faith so firm endeared him to God's heart,
Led kings to think that Sarah's not his wife, to save his part.
Old Noah, after riding out the flood in ark, we see,
In saving men and beast, got drunk, disgraced his family.

And Jonah tried to run and hide, escape God's holy will.
King David sinned: he lusted for Uriah's wife, him killed.
And Moses slew a man; in anger struck the Rock too hard.
Three times did Peter say he didn't know Christ Jesus, Lord.

In spite of sins, God used each one of these to work His plan.
Each did repent, turned back to God, and he forgave each man!
If He can use cracked vessels such as these (you see, He does)
Then surely He can use our broken ones, use even us!

What matters too, is not just cracks, but what's inside the pots,
For each of us is cracked, we see; and this is what God's got.
He used those vessels, though so badly cracked was every one,
And He can even mend the cracks when we accept His Son!

September 12, 1996

Creation

From NOTHING God created all:
The earth and the seas and the mountains tall.
He made flowers, grass, and trees;
He made amoebas, whales and bees.

He made the sun and moon and stars;
He placed them there, both near and far.
He made all things to work together--
Each unit, even all the weather.

In His own image He made man,
To worship Him, commune as we can.
And He made angels, heavenly beings;
They have their duties for God, we're seeing.

Incomprehensible to us
With simple minds, so we must trust.
We know that God's book tells the truth
About all things--we must have faith.

We praise our Father's holy name,
Are blessed and thankful, us He claims.
We worship our Creator now;
In total awe before him bow.

August 10, 2002

Escape

When things go wrong, we try to run
By blaming others--anyone.
From problems we do try to hide,
Because of selfish stubborn pride.

But as we run from place to place,
And job to job to "save our face,"
We find the things we can't escape
Are always there, seemed to us taped.

Although it's sometimes others' fault,
More often, ours--more so than not.
We see it's WE who need to change
In many ways--there's quite a range!

With Jesus in our lives we'd be
More kind and patient, happy, free.
And then there'd be no need to run
From anything or anyone.

October 30, 1996

Five Seasons Of Life

Spring:

In springtime of life we spring forth from the womb;
We learn and are taught, and we grow very soon.
As blades of green grass or some young lily sprouts,
Young children are tender, and learn as we're taught.

Summer:

In summer we grow and mature as we bloom,
We produce and we nurture new life as it comes,
Becoming whatever we're destined to be
To benefit mankind and aid society.

Autumn:

In autumn of life we will reap what we sowed
In work and improvements and life as it flowed.
And teaching the young ones of life and the Father,
How important it is to love God and each other.

Winter:

In winter we rest when our hair looks like snow;
Our bodies decrease in their vigor, go glow.
We enjoy our grandchildren, and even some "greats;"
If we granted more years, we can know those born late.

Eternity:

And then comes the time to graduate into heaven.

We pray we've fulfilled our work here, and have given

To others the love of our Maker above,

And helped them know firmly God's Son and His love.

June 2, 2002

Garden of my Heart

I have a garden you cannot see:
It's in my heart inside of me.
It's filled with friendships sweet and dear
With those I love both far and near.

Some are family, some are friends;
My love for them just never ends;
And each, my precious jewel treasures,
Has value with no way to measure.

My plants, adorned with jewel flowers,
Give joyful love for many hours;
Yet, now I see there in the center
There's One much brighter and more tender.

It is the One Who died for me--
Who paid my debt at Calvary.
His name is Jesus: He is mine,
And also yours, oh see Him shine!

For Jesus, in the center space,
Makes all the garden a special place,
As every other jewel flower
Depends for brightness on His power.

God Loves Each One

While parked along the town's main street,
See many people different shapes.
There some are large and some are small;
And some are short and some are tall.

See some round bellies over belts;
And some flat tummies could be felt.
Some have long necks, are very tall;
Some seem to have no neck at all.

Some have short legs, and some have long;
And so their arms do match along.
See ears and noses, hands and feet:
They all are different; it's so neat!

God made us all made every one.
We're His creations, we're his own.
So every person's made unique,
In character and color, cheeks.

Yet even twins are not alike;
He made us each the way He likes,
To fill a place that's just for us
That's in His plan, so let's say "yes"

To His great plan, and for our place
To work together in God's grace.
Each one is God's own special treasure,
For He loves each one without measure.

God's Greatest Gift

Yes, God is love, but God is just.
God made mankind and gave to us
The world as home, and gift of choice;
But Adam sinned; Christ paid the price.

When Jesus died upon that cross,
Disciples thought 'twas greatest loss.
Instead, it was greatest gain
For all mankind, in spite of pain.

For this is Father's greatest gift.
Each must accept it, for a lift
Into God's arms, forever safe
To live with Him in blissful state.

So if you haven't Him received,
Please do not wait. Be not deceived:
The only way to be made whole
Is give to God your heart and soul!

April 25, 2003

Guilt Crossed Out

Oh why do we insist on wasting energy on guilt--
Because we have a conscience, that's the way we were built?
But only Laws that God has made, and man's that do relate,
Would be the ones we should obey to keep contented state.

Now after disobeying God, my conscience says it's wrong.
I asked God, "Please forgive;" He does and then I praise with song.
What right have I to hold a grudge 'gainst self or anyone
When holy, perfect God Himself forgives--so quick it's done!

God will forgive His children our mistakes if we but ask;
He promised in His holy book He'll quickly do the task;*
For that's why Jesus Christ, God's perfect Son came here and died:
He paid the awful price--Crossed out our guilt, was CRUCIFIED.

If we insist on wallowing in guilt for sin that's paid,
We hurt ourselves, and also we insult what God has said.
If we accept His greatest gift, our guilt is total waste;
We only ask him to forgive; and then He does, with haste.

And joyful we can be, as wasting no more time or pain
On totally uncalled-for guilt, according to God's plan.
Of course we ask God's help to keep us on the narrow way,
So we may stray less often, growing nearer Him each day.

*1 John 1:9 (paraphrased)

Heaven

How wholly awesome it will be
To spend quite all eternity
With God, the Father, Son and Spirit
There in heaven living in it!

To be with God, the great Creator,
Worship Him in all His splendor,
See Him, talk full face to face--
The One Who loves us, grants us grace!

How beautiful and problem-free
With endless joy and ecstasy,
Throughout all time with Christ, to be--
No pain or tears or sadness see.

There'll be no sorrow, trials, death.
Our dear ones: family, friends, of faith,
Will be united with our Lord:
We know, because of God's firm word!

There streets of gold, and sparkling gems
Adorn the buildings on the beams;
Jerusalem in holy light,
And from God's throne the River of Life.

There is no night, no need for sun,
For God gives light to everyone.
The Tree of Life grows different fruit:
A kind each month, all tastes will suit.

But only God's own children rate
To enter in those pearly gates.
And all do worship God on high.
We join in praise, sing "Alleluia!"

To be God's child, accept His Son,
Believe in Him, the Holy One.
Accept His gift so freely given,
And spend eternity in heaven!
April 17, 2000

Let Go and Let God

Dear Father, we're sorry we cling to our troubles,
For You are our God, and to keep them makes double.
We think we can handle our problems the best,
But we only fumble and make a big mess.

If only we'd give all our problems to You
And trust You to solve them the way You can do
(You told us You'd solve them and things would be better,
For You are much wiser), we wouldn't be fretters.

Please strengthen our faith so in You we will trust;
For You're in control, and You even made us!
For You there is nothing too difficult to do,
And love is your essence; we should trust only you.

So let us have faith to let go and let God
Handle our problems; just give them to the Lord.

October 20,1998

Marriage Advice

Marriage advice, now is that your request?
Yes, we have been married, passed sixty-year test.
Together as one with our own chosen dears,
And still growing closer now, all through the years.

The primary thing we would say to you two:
Keep Jesus the center of all that you do!
Do always consider the other's desire
Before your own wishes, or pride that's on fire.

At first you should choose the right one just for you.
Compatible always in all that you do.
Come into your marriage determined to stay.
It always will last if intended this way.

Self-control is a must to be used; it is right
Whenever two people disagree, so don't fight.
Be patient and kind, remain peaceful and calm.
And share in the duties and pleasures of home.

Keep bright happy attitude; laugh at yourself.
Some matters are not worth a fuss—"blow them off!"
Do help one another with interests as well,
With worship and service, and hobbies, we tell.

In making decisions of major import,
Consult well together, in wisdom deport.*
Important to share just what's down in your heart;
To understand other's deep feelings is smart.

Be quick to forgive, or apology make,
And try understanding; the other's side take.
The Bible says don't let the sun to go down
Before a quarrel's settled; do smile and don't frown.

No person is perfect, not I and not you,
So two who are married must see this as true.
Keep loving each other in spite of those faults,
And keep growing closer, and never apart.

Be constant true to your chosen good mate,
For, first here on earth, he (she) always must rate.
So now, main advice that we have for you two:
Keep Jesus the center of all that you do!

And pray every day!
Tom and Rowena 2003
*Act

Marvelous Creation

A wondrous creation, humanity--"man!"
Created by God, as only He can.
Of body and mind and spirit we're made.
The spirit and mind live when body's decayed.

God made every part to fulfill its own task
What more is there, then, that we ever can ask?
A central control, a computer sans equal,
A mind, many parts that don't need a sequel.

We're mobile and thinking, our hands can do so much.
We see, hear and smell, also feel what we touch.
Digestion does fuel our bodies so well,
But we must be careful what's put into cells.

Yes, man is a marvelous, wondrous creation.
God spoke, and He made us from his own imagination,
In His image made us to worship and love Him.
Forever with Him, and never above Him.

We're told to be kind to earth's many dumb creatures,
And we're to take care of this fine garden's features.
Forgive us, dear Lord, for we've made it a mess.
Our greed and stupidity, sin we confess.

Please give us the wisdom to follow, obey You,
So all of your creatures can worship, enjoy you.
January 10, 2002

Satan Laughs

Now Satan roams both day and night,
And stirs up pride, dissension, fright.
Just any time he can, he keeps
God's people from their God-- nor weeps!
HE LAUGHS his wicked laugh with glee.

Oh how he loves to drive a wedge
And push the Christians to the edge
By disagreements, hurt, or pride
To make them all curl up inside.
Oh, how he laughs with wicked glee!

And interest of the worldly sort
Keep people far away, apart
From loving Christians of strong faith,
So, inch by inch, they move.
And Satan laughs vigorously.

To break God's people all apart
So there's no fellowship of heart
Make Satan so ecstatic that
He keeps right on a-doing that.
And laughing wickedly with glee.

When Christians stay apart--alone,
They miss God's love that can be shown.
They miss the strength of fellows' faith.
Instruction, love, and warm embrace.
So Satan laughs on wickedly.

Then Satan knows he's winning souls
Away from God, which is his goal.
So if you're one who stays away,
Rejoin, and don't give him his way!
And don't let Satan laugh at you.

April 28, 2003

Smile; Don't Complain

It does no good to worry, cry,
or even to complain,
When problems or infirmities
are causing us some pain.
It's better just to smile or laugh,
and see the funny side.
Somehow the pains affect us less
if we push them aside.

Example: when I'm shaky
and I spill my glass of juice,
To laugh and say, "Oh now I'm cool!"
would be a good excuse.
Or if my back is hurting much,
I'd even laugh and say,
"Oh, I'm just lazy now," and so
I'd pass it off this way.

Therefore it's always better just
to keep the moment light
Than being miserable all day;
let's try to keep it bright.
'Cause others do not wish to share
our misery with us;
They'd much prefer to hear us laugh
than make a great big fuss!

July 2, 2003

The Lighthouse

God's Word's a stable Lighthouse
Lighting well the rocky way:
It guides the feet of little ones
By night as well as day.
We need it for ourselves, you see,
As well as for the young
Let's teach them how to find the Lord,
Stay far away from wrong.

For those who do not know God's
Holy book, His Word,
And anyone not privileged
To know our precious Lord,
Then WE must learn to be a lighthouse
Showing them the way
To walk the path of life they should
By night as well as day.

We must reflect the light
Of our Creator's holy Word
To guide them to the True Light Source—
To find and know the Lord.

The Sun Stood Still

Oh Joshua and the Israelites
Were fighting all the Amorites.
The Lord sent hail, and vict'ry gave
To Israel's men that special day.

That very day did Joshua pray,
"Please let the sun and moon to stay
And not at all to move along,
So that this day Thou wilt prolong."

So God did honor that request:
The sun and moon stood still in rest--
Prolonged that day, so Israel won
The battle with five kings as one!

Joshua 10:11-14
March 23,1997

Trouble = Opportunities

Not all have problems, all have pain.
Some people cry and some, complain.
But some will smile and see the good,
To lighten up and change the mood.

Our troubles can be opportunities
To help us all find serenity
By knowing God is in control;
Good attitudes we then will hold.

With lemons, some will make a "face;"
Some make a pie that's sweet to taste;
And some will make good lemonade
To share with other lads and maids.

Bad times are like the lemon, see.
Our choices makes what our lives will be:
Be sad, or live more happily?
What is our attitude to be?

Your choice and mine--which will it be?

Nature

Butterflies

When butterflies are on the wing,
We know that surely it is spring,
Because they need the flowers to live;
Both need the sunshine, beauty give.

At first the egg, and then the worm
Devouring many leaves in turn.
We find it spins a blanket soon
To sleep inside it's own cocoon.

Inside, a miracle takes place:
The earthbound worm is soon replaced
By lovely wing-ed one of grace!
We watch it flit about the place.

Transformed, made new, this lovely creature,
God's special miracle of nature,
Shows how He even changes me:
With spiritual birth he sets me free!

May 16, 1996

Copperhead!

In days of yore when I was young,
did tricks up on a rope
That stretched between two trees
out in the hills. I didn't stop
Until my mother called me in
for supper; in a blink,
It happened oh, so fast--I hardly
had the time to think.

Then there I was, midair, while going down
toward the ground.
I saw, coiled right below me there,
a thing: long and thin and brown!
So quick, I don't know how--
an angel must have helped me up:
No other way, so sudden, found myself
back ON THAT ROPE!

I promptly yelled with all my strength,
expressed my certain dread.
My daddy came with hoe in hand
and killed that copperhead.
And now, consider what a miracle
event that surely was.
God showed His love, protected me.
You see, He really does!

May 12, 2000

Dog Apology

Two doggie beds sitting there side by side
For two black Chihuahuas to sleep inside,
For Robin and Shadow were two Chihuahua friends.
Now Robin was papa of Shadow. Once when
Son Shadow did something that Dad did offend,
Their master told Shadow to apologize then.

But little did Master know Shadow understood!
For he was surprised when he saw Shadow's mood.
Young Shadow put tail and head down to the floor,
Slunk all the way BACKWARD through Robin's front door!

I'm sure Papa accepted the apology then,
For all became normal and they were again friends.

July 20, 2002

Doves

Two gently white doves in our home
fly about.
Their voices are soft and their
manner is tame;
They trust us completely, and
never fly about.
(We always must watch where we step,
not to maim.)

I never have seen gentle doves
that would fight;
They seek for companionship,
coo, and cuddle up.
They share all their food and the
nest, where alight;
Our doves never argue, even
share with the pup.

The Bible says doves were sent
out from the ark
To seek for some evidence
showing dry land
When waters receded, so
Noah could park;
For doves are home-loving,
return to their man.

A dove represented Holy Spirit
of God;
When Jesus was baptized--the Spirit
of Love
Descended on Jesus
as only It could
Identify Who is the
Son from above.

February 7, 1994

Hamsters

Two funny hamster "teddy bears"
Amused us, chased away our cares.
They slept in shredded paper nest
That they had made in which to rest.

There in the wheel they ran all night
And rattled, played, would cardboard bite.
Oh they were fun to cuddle, watch,
But sometimes very hard to catch.

One little hamster ran away,
Was loose and free for many days.
Oh, it was close to ninety days
Before we found his hiding place.

We came upon a chewed-out hole
Through twenty dresses on a pole.
So with detective work we did,
We found that hamster, where he hid.

And then he joined his lonely mate,
Could eat real food, also be safe
From cats and dogs back in his cage--
Big dangers he had failed to gauge.

January 20 , 1996

Handicap

A String quartet was playing
lovely music around;
We heard them in the best museum
of our little town.
A pesky fly was buzzing 'round,
alit upon the nose
Of each one of the players,
as the notes arose.

Fast as they played, then slowly
and sometimes a welcome rest.
Persistent was that fly,
although 'twas brushed off nose and vest.
As perspiration glowed upon those
players' furrowed brows,
Attractive to the fly,
he flew from each one's brow to nose.

An upwardly directed stream
of air was blown from mouth:
It only made him move a bit,
alight and settle south.
Both hands of every player there
were busy constantly,
Which made it very difficult
to concentrate and play.

Phenomenal it was, you see,

that concert was complete--

And really played so very well;

it was a special treat.

Deserved applause was given

to the players, and here's why:

They overcame a handicap--

that sticky pesky fly!

May 19, 1996

Lost Iguana

To give his young lizard some freedom one night,
It's owner did let it ride sitting upright
Upon his left shoulder about the whole house;
But that green iguana jumped off and ran loose.

At last he was found and restored to his place
On owner's left shoulder, but friend changed the pace.
Before the teenagers went out on the town,
We couldn't determine where lizard could be found.

Before we retired for the rest of the night,
We searched the whole room with our trusty flashlight.
We shined it behind and between and below
Just all of the things in the room we could show.

Reluctantly all went to bed for the night,
But searched for that lizard again with dawn light.
Surprise of surprises! Upon Christmas tree
One cold green iguana was looking at me!

December 17, 1996

Majestic Eagle

Majestic eagle, flying high,
You freely roam about the sky,
You dip and soar as up you fly,
So trusting there, without a try.

Your wings just open in a spread,
And on the current make your bed.
You ride in the air on up and down,
The circle more and on around.

It looks so effortless and fun,
It makes me wish that I could run
And just take off and join you there
A mile or so up in the air.

You seem to be so in control:
In spite of gravity, your soul
Is free as you survey the land
With eyes that see the small or grand.

To represent our so-great land,
I've come to see and understand
Why you were chosen above all others:
Your spirit's free and high, flies further.

For that's the spirit of our land:
No limits can be set to stand;
For we are always reaching higher,
Achieving more, just like you, flyer.

You set example in your trust
As you depend upon the thrust
Of currents in the upper air—
So we must trust in God, to dare.

When storms below you earth do threaten,
You even rise above toward heaven;
So we can live above life's storms
By resting in God's loving arms.

God's prophet said it isn't hard,
Our spirits to soar—just trust the Lord.
Then we can live as strong and free:
As you are there, so we can be.

(Isaiah 40:31)

Man's Best Friends

Oh, we can learn much from our dear canine friends,
For they have good character traits that they lend.
They're loyal, devoted, courageous, and patient;
They exercise judgment; are cheerful, obedient.

They're accepting of all circumstances they're in;
And show sense of humor, play jokes on their kin.
Alertness is always a trait that helps man,
For dogs can hear noises that we hardly can.

They smell many odors that we can't detect,
Alert us sometimes, and from dangers protect.
They're sensitive always to feelings and moods,
And sympathize warmly with joy or with gloom.

They warn us of dangers, and save many lives;
They find many lost in disasters and ice.
They work, pulling sleds and retrieving the game
That hunters have shot in their efforts at same.

Dogs guard many places, keep safe where there's need;
They're eyes for the blind; for the deaf, ears to heed.
In cold winter time, they keep so warm
When heat is much needed, prevent freezing harm

They also chase rodents and other known pests,

Are brave, sacrificial, in times of great tests.

So dogs are quite often called "best friends of man:"

Companions and helpers, as only they can.

July 27, 2004

Music In Nature

There's music everywhere we go:
In woods and fields and streams and snow.
The birds do sing in hills and trees;
They feed their babies, never cease.

They're calling to their rightful mates
To find each other in their place.
Also, the moose and whales call theirs;
And crickets, wolves, and wooly bears.

Most creatures need not be alone,
So seek to be among their own.
So fish look for their kind to mate,
Their species so to propagate.

Frogs are croaking, calling too,
They play their "fiddles" in their slough.
The babbling brooks and waterfalls
Do sing as well, and never stall.

The zephyrs turn to breezes; storms
Blow whistling through the rocks and thorns.
When autumn leaves turn orange and red,
They swirl toward their winter beds.

The soft and glistening snowflakes fall,

As silently they stack up tall.

Too many cause a branch to crack,

And loud it sounds a great big "whack:"

Percussion's added to the sounds of nature's music all around.

So, Tunes with harmony beneath,

Also percussion for the beat

Combine for nature's music here,

Just as a sample on our sphere.

Springtime Is Fall

Most trees lose their leaves in the Autumn, called "Fall,"
But live Oaks are different: Springtime is their "Fall."
In Springtime the leaves of the live Oaks fall down;
They dance and they swirl as they leap toward the ground.

All winter these beautiful trees have been green
While others were barren--no leaves could be seen.
In Springtime most plants will awaken and grow:
The ones that were sleeping, the live Oaks also.

These latter ones mentioned just don't rest so long,
Because they must hurry, catch up and be strong.
They bloom while still shedding and growing new leaves.
What other big trees have to hurry like these?

March 18, 1995

Tiny Helicopters
(Happy Hummers)

Their wings are beating there so fast
That we can't even see them pass:
Fly up and down and forward, back--
Maneuverability, no lack!

A work of art with feathers bright,
With long curved beaks and bodies slight,
They're always watching, so alert,
With quick reaction, very pert.

It's fun to watch them play their games
With lively friends who are the same,
Alighting on the feeder red
Or hov'ring, bobbing overhead.

How happy they; they're playing games.
In sipping nectar, perfect aims
With beaks, and flight through big oak tree:
How marvelous, God's creatures free!

They hover while they put their beaks
Into the flowers, nectar seek,
Because their bodies need the sweets
For energy for fast wing beats.

One angles sharply, darting down
Within a foot of solid ground;
Then sharply turns on upturned flight;
Reverse path exactly right.

I see them there; before I think,
They're gone again just in a blink.
I see them darting 'round and 'round,
And off again--the nectar found!

When resting on the near clothesline,
They look like clothespins many times,
Because they are that very size
And outline there against the skies.

Sometimes on very long migrations,
Traveling far across the nations,
Hitching rides with goose's feathers:
Friends agree to go together!

Oh, hummingbirds are charming friends,
Like tiny 'copters in the wind.
Our God made them for perfect flight,
So versatile and very light.
January 1999 - August 2000

Toad's Spaghetti

I walked around the block and searched for bugs down on the road;
I found some rolly-pollies for our hungry little toad.
Because the ground was wet from rain, there were some fishing worms
That crawled out on the street, did wiggle, flop and squirm.

I gathered all the bugs and worms I found to feed our toad,
And put them in a small glass jar--they made a wiggly load.
When Toad observed his tasty meal upon the floor of cage,
He perked right up, shot out his tongue, the perfect distance gauged.

Like magic, rolly-pollies disappeared into our toad's big mouth;
But fishing worms took longer--like spaghetti, slid from south.

August 21, 1999

Velcro Pup

She's closer than a shadow,
Almost closer than my skin.
She stays right here beside me
all through thick and even thin.
She tries to guess just where I'm going,
then she hurries there;
She dashes to another room,
and even up the stair.

If I sit down to read awhile
or work there at the desk,
She's right beside me looking up,
or nudging me to ask,
"I want to be with you, whatever you do,
please take me up?"
So that's my Goldie,* buddy mine;
I call her "Velcro Pup."

She sets a fine example for us
humans with our Lord;
For we should stick to Him, like velcro,
and obey His word.
If we would follow Him always,
forever looking up,
We'd not fall down; He'd lift us up,
as I do Velcro Pup.

July 15, 2003
*Chihuahua

Philosophy

Agape Love

Now, "What is love?: is deep to ponder.
It's not just something "way out yonder;"
But it's experienced in ways we think,
Our words and deeds-- there is a link.

God's kind of love: be patient, kind,
And share with others a gentle mind.
Remember, pride and self are last
If with God's love we do our tasks.

"Agape" is the term we use
To show a caring point of view--
Even with all the other kinds of love,
It binds us close to God above.

To see another through God's eyes
And understand a friend, is wise.
For "God is love," His word declares
And so we know He really cares!

No greater love can any give
Than giving life so we may live;
For that is why Christ Jesus died,
And for our sins was crucified.

September 16, 1993

Birthdays

In days gone by when I was small,
A birthday was great fun for all.
With great anticipation then,
Each year marked growth, so said my kin.

Then came the time I wished to stay
Just twenty-nine forever—aye!
Don't count them up, just celebrate
Each year upon that certain date.

They used to measure height each year
To find my growth from "there" to "here."
But if they'd measure me these days,
They'd find I've grown in other ways!
(Instead of UP and all about,
So now it's DOWN and wider OUT!)

Then come the time when we are glad
And thankful for each year we've had.
No matter what the number, this—
Take it above what else there is!!

Center Pole

Just as a tent must have
a center pole to keep it up,
So must each family home have strength
from bottom to the top.
With Jesus as our Center Pole
to keep our home upright,
We know it will withstand the storms
through every day and night.

As each one grows much closer, then,
to Jesus and the others
They're growing closer to the Same:
and learn to love all others.
And as each one holds closer to
the mighty Center Pole,
It follows then as day the night,
the family will hold.

Observing the differences between families that know and rely
on Jesus Christ and those that do not, inspired me to write
this poem. Our home has had Jesus as our "Center Pole" for
the many years of our marriage, and He has kept us strong
and happy. For this we praise and thank Him. We pray this
will help many other families everywhere to be happy, loving,
and strong by keeping Jesus in the center of their likes.

Children Are Loaned

How blessed are we to have been loaned
Four children such as these,
Belonging as they do to God
We've spent time on our knees
While seeking wisdom, patience, help,
In teaching them to love
And know their heavenly Father God,
To worship Him above.

They've been a very sacred trust;
We dedicated them
So very early in their lives
To serve and live for Him.
All four have come to know and love
Our Father and His Son;
And now they teach their children
Salvation has been won.

They all do know from whence they came
and what they're here to do;
And joyous are our family
for loving Jesus, too.
January 7, 1993

Days Of My Life

The eighth of October we call this new day;
I thank the good Lord for it now, and I pray
To use it for His so-great glory-- for Him;
So I must not waste it, a precious new gem.

And now as I ponder the days long gone by--
So many short years of them into the sky--
They're made up of days, given one and by one,
Each sunup and sundown for work and for fun.

At first as a baby, two parents were given
When I was a cherub just freshly from heaven--
Dependant was I on their wisdom and care,
But grew independent, the world I could dare.

Then school, university, marriage: the ways
I spent the next sixteen whole years full of days.
Still young, filled with pep, we did set a good pace
And raised four fine children who seek for Thy face.

And after our children were out on their own,
Our parents were needing our help there alone;
So most of our days a few years were then spent
A-caring for parents when they were dependant.

As looking way back over the years' full days,
I wonder if how I have used them always
Has been very pleasing to God up above--
The minutes, the hours, and the days--filled with love?

For there's an accounting that's yet to be made
To God on his throne when we meet, to be said.
So far as I know, there's a little more time
To live the remainder--in His will abide.

Lord, give me the wisdom, the patience, the strength,
Obedient to Thee must I be the full length
Of every divine precious gift of a day
Thou givest to me; may I serve Thee always.

October 8, 1991

Forgive!

Let pride not block the way:
forgiveness grant, and seek;
But humble be, and think the best,
even turn the other cheek.

Sept. 1, 1993

"Never" And "Always"

Are "never" and "always" some words we can use?
We often discover exceptions to the rules
As stated by people like you and like me.
Can absolute words truly absolute be?

Now only two things can we be certain of:
The first is: man changes, does constantly move;
And second--eternal and always secure--
That God is *Unchanging*, of this we are sure!

These two profound facts, the exceptions they be,
To "never say 'never' or 'always,'" you see.
So, yes, we CAN say that man ALWAYS does change,
And God NEVER changes, gives peace through each age.

August 30, 1994

How God Loves Us!

Our heavenly Father has made us, we know,
To praise Him and worship Him, learn and to grow
In every possible way more like Him,
Commune with our God who forgives every sin.

He loves us so much we cannot conceive
Of that kind of love: and we must it receive!
He sent His dear Jesus, the only pure One
To die on the cross--our forgiveness He won!

To know our great father, we love Him so much;
And He'll never leave us and never lose touch!
He knows all about us (in awe we do kneel):
Our innermost thoughts and our trials, what we feel.

There are no mere words to express what I feel
Of gratitude, love, and protection so real.
When troubles overwhelm me, my Father's right here;
I reach up to touch, Him, and me he does cheer.

Although He already does know everything,
I talk it over with God, to Him cling.
My Counselor, Father, my Comfort and my strength--
By him I will stay my whole life, the full length.

September 22, 1992

Mother To My Parents

Our roles became reversed, Mom dear,
as you were growing old:
For as a babe in arms, you see,
you cared for me, I'm told.
But then when I was middle-aged,
and you were helpless there,
And could not work or even walk
or leave your blue wheelchair;
Then I assume the mother role
to you, my mother dear,
Because you could not care for self
(like baby me), it's clear.

With love you did all of the things
for baby me you must;
Then lovingly I cared for you
(yes, me you had to trust.)
It must be very difficult
to be no longer free,
But prisoner in a chair or bed:
you were there reluctantly.

Then, Daddy dear, it was your turn:
you needed me to come.
So then I cared for you awhile,
till God did call you home.
You even called me "Mother" when
I cared for you in love:
You were aware our roles were changed,
reversed as planned above.

Now each is freed from body prison,
called by God above,
Your family here does miss you so,
remembers all your love.

So when my body or my mind
is wearing out and weak,
I pray my children love enough
that wisdom they will seek,
To see that I am well-cared-for
if helpless I become;
Though NEVER do I wish to burden
any happy home!
Febuary 3, 1992

Only One

Each one of us is only one,
So what can one of us have won
When all is said and all is done--
When all our races have been run?

You'd be surprised what one can do
That counts for much for all of you.
Consider some who have done much,
With good in mind, and kindly touch.

Take Mother Theresa and Jonas Salk
Whose actions speak much more than talk.
And there are many, many others
Who can be named who help their brothers.

So that's the key to doing much:
To be unselfish, kind; for such
Their attitude has always been
To help mankind, as we have seen.

But there is One Who changed the world
As history has come unfurled--
Guess Who?! Yes, Jesus is the One
Who makes the difference, God's only Son!

August 30, 1991

Sonflowers

We learn from the sunflower's natural way;
It follows the sunshine throughout the whole day,
And energy gains from its power so bright.
So we should be SONflowers, with eyes on Christ's light.
As SONflowers, we need to follow the SON,
Receive of HIS power 'til our day is done.

September 10, 1993

This Too Will Pass

"This too will pass," it's oft been told,
and proved to be advice worth gold.
For now we know from life's events
That it is true—it all makes sense!

The circumstances change always:
Those times we think are our worst days
Will fade away and then we praise
Our God, and we our voices raise.

Unbearable the circumstance;
But if we pray, give God a chance,
He'll guide us through the highs and lows,
Bring victory with his love that flows.

Believe this fact: "this too will pass!"
We'll be survivors, winners, yes!
And stronger in our living faith
For trusting God, on Him to wait.

January 21, 1995

Unique

Oh, who is perfect? Not you nor I!
And though we look both low and high,
We'll never find one knowing all;
And no-one's skills are perfect at ALL.

Perhaps you're better when you teach;
Another, better at the beach.
Still others may excel at sports;
Or yet another's a lawyer of sorts.

Created in God's image, we:
The way God wants us each to be,
Yet each unique and loved the same:
Forgiven, saved by Jesus' Name.

Each one has gifts from God above;
It's up to us to use them in love.
Each has his own unique good place
To fit God's plan, live in His grace.

So you are not inferior to me,
And I will not beneath you be;
Because we're different by plan
To work together as we can.

Wise Parenting

Parents, remember that children so dear
Have ideas, and feelings of joy, love and fear,
They're persons with needs; body, mind and soul
That's growing: let nurturing love be the goal.

Let parents keep open their hearts and minds.
And listen, use judgment, be firm, but be kind.
Give reasons for judgments, as "welfare of all,"
Or measured by "laws of our God over all."

"Provoke not the children to anger," said the Lord,
"But teach them to love and obey our God's Word."*
"Be righteously angry, controlling yourself,
And let not the sun set till all wrath is squelched."**

Do listen, stay calm, and be reasonable, fair;
And pray for God's wisdom, with love always care;
And a good example for children to 'mime;
(A good sense of humor's an asset oft-times!)

* Ephesians 6:4 (paraphrased)
** Ephesians 4:26 (paraphrased)

July 30, 1995

Worry

Now what is the profit to spend time in worry?
So if you can change things, then do it, and hurry.
But if there is nothing at all you can do,
It won't help to worry, or even to "stew."

It never does help matters, only does harm,
And even brings illness and causes alarm.
According to scripture, to worry is sin:
'Tis true, we have found worry never does win.

Instead, we should take our concerns to the Lord;
For him, it is proven, there's nothing too hard!
So let the Lord Jesus give us His good peace:
Give Him all our burdens, our worries release.

September 26, 1991

About the Author

Rowena Stenis was born in Norman, Oklahoma in 1922, and her early years were filled with dinnertime talk about words, language, and their usage. She attended public school in Austin, Texas before attending The University of Texas, where she graduated with high honors in the Music Department. While at UT, she met her husband, Tom, who, like the author, was a member of the UT Symphony Orchestra. Mr. and Mrs. Stenis have been married for nearly 70 years, having raised 4 children who, in turn produced 14 grandchildren and 9 great-grandchildren. Both Rowena and Tom Stenis are now retired and continue to reside in Texas and play in musical groups.

Mrs. Stenis has enjoyed a respected career as a teacher of music, both privately and in the Texas school system. She has directed choirs in the churches they attended. Her interests include the establishment and maintenance of the tradition of "Camp Gramps", an annual week of family fun.

On their retirement from the Lubbock Symphony after 40 years, Mr. and Mrs. Stenis were honored by a standing ovation from both the audience and the orchestra. They received a similar honor when, after 20 years, they retired from playing in the Austin Civic Orchestra.

Mrs. Stenis has had her poetry published in local periodicals and newsletters. This is her second published book.